M000202228

THE

FRAME FORMULA

*Your Parenting Source to Communicate
Like It's Your Superpower!*

Lydia Taggart

Copyright © 2019 Lydia Taggart and Taggart Trainings.

ALL RIGHTS RESERVED. No part of this book or its associated ancillary materials may be reproduced or transmitted in any form or by any means, electronic or mechanical, including photocopying, recording, or by any informational storage or retrieval system without explicit written permission from the publisher.

PUBLISHED BY Taggart Trainings
Paperback ISBN 978-0-578-59421-7

DISCLAIMER AND/OR LEGAL NOTICES
While all attempts have been made to verify information provided in this book and its ancillary materials, neither the author or publisher assumes any responsibility for errors, inaccuracies or omissions and is not responsible for any financial loss by customer in any manner. Any slights of people or organizations are unintentional. If advice concerning legal, financial, accounting or related matters is needed, the services of a qualified professional should be sought. This book and its associated ancillary materials, including verbal and written training, is not intended for use as a source of legal, financial, or accounting advice. You should be aware of the various laws governing business transactions or other business practices in your particular geographical locations.

EARNINGS & INCOME DISCLAIMER
With respect to the reliability, accuracy, timeliness, usefulness, adequacy, completeness, and/or suitability of information provided in this book, Lydia Taggart, Taggart Trainings, its partners, associates, affiliates, consultants, and/or presenters make no warranties, guarantees, representations, or claims of any kind. Readers' results will vary depending on a number of factors. Any and all claims or representations as to income earnings are not to be considered average earnings. Testimonials are not representative. This book and all products and services are for educational and informational purposes only. Use caution and see the advice of qualified professionals. Check with your accountant, attorney or professional advisor before acting on this or any information. You agree that Lydia Taggart, and/or Taggart Trainings are not responsible for the success or failure of your personal, business, health or financial decisions related to any information presented by Lydia Taggart, Taggart Trainings or company products or services. Earnings potential is entirely dependent on the efforts, skills, and application of the individual person. Any examples, stories, references, or case studies are for illustrative purposes only and should not be interpreted as testimonies and/or examples of what reader and/or consumers can generally expect from the information. No representation in any part of this information materials and/or seminar training are guarantees or promises for actual performance. Any statements, strategies, concepts, techniques, exercises and ideas in the information, materials and/or seminar training offered are simply opinion or experience, and thus should not be misinterpreted as promises, typical results or guarantees (expressed or implied). The author and publisher (Lydia Taggart, Taggart Trainings nor any of their representatives) shall in no way, under any circumstances, be held liable to any party (or third party) for any direct, indirect, punitive, special, incidental or other consequential damages arising directly or indirectly from any use of books, materials and/or seminar trainings, which is provided "as is," and without warranties.

PRINTED IN THE UNITED STATES OF AMERICA

I dedicate this book to my husband, Steve, for more than I can say, and to our children. Without them there would be nothing. They have taught me everything I know.

Anything else I have sought to learn is because of them.

Your bonus for investing in

THE FRAME FORMULA

Your Parenting Source to Communicate Like It's Your Superpower!

Special FREE Bonus Gift for YOU!

To help you achieve better communication immediately, you are invited to go to: TaggartTrainings.com

Register for YOUR FREE 30-Minute Super Hero Coaching Session

FREE $997 VALUE

TaggartTrainings.com

LYDIA TAGGART

CONTENTS

INTRODUCTION

They were expected to spend time in the Neonatal Intensive Care Unit (NICU). Being a quadruplet will do that to you. I was happy as their mother to see them progressing, living. They were not able to be held much because they were having trouble regulating their body temperature and the breathing tubes got in the way. But they were growing and learning how to eat and breathe on their own. Yes, I was happy and hopeful.

Naturally everyone in our church was helping care for our family and they were all eager for an update on the babies' progress. I told the women how each one was progressing. As I spoke of the breathing tubes being removed for an hour I could feel my cheeks glowing with joy.

One way or another, they were going to make it.

As soon as the report was completed another woman shared about her needs for extra help and prayers. He grandson was not doing well and was also in the NICU. Her expression was full of tears, worry and sorrow. The contrast between our two experiences in the same place with similar circumstances, but so different emotionally, struck me very strongly. Why was I able to express joy and love and she was full of sorrow in her love?

It was our frame of reference, or our point of view, that influenced our reactions. That frame of reference is a FRAME that is always there.

Always. It is always there whether or not we use it intentionally. It is always underlying the way we interact with ourselves and the world around us.

There are different types of frames. A frame for a house is what the rest of the building is structured around. It supports the rest of the building and is built on the foundation as part of the beginning phase of construction.

Eye glasses have a frame the holds the lenses in place. This frame supports the unique needs for the vision of the wearer. When a pair of glasses is purchased it is actually a frame and lenses that are later put together to make the pair of glasses.

A picture frame adds value to what's inside it. Often what's inside a frame is a picture of a family. I remember when we had family pictures taken when our kids were young. It was quite an ordeal to get all six of our children to cooperate and I was excited to display the results of our efforts. The pictures were affordable and I asked the photographer to add a frame. It would make it possible for me to actually display our picture. When I got the bill I was shocked at how much the frame had cost. The value the frame added was more than expected but without it the picture would be nearly worthless, unable to be displayed or appreciated.

It's through frames that we can appreciate life's experiences. I remember my mother telling me to take a mental photograph on several occasions. The image of a fish swimming around my feet while I stood in a clear pond, my bare feet feeling the smooth stone beneath me. Grandpa, a few feet away standing beneath the waterfall. The rush of water splashing off his shoulders. That moment captured and has influenced how I live my life. Memories form perspectives forever ingrained in my brain because I have intentionally put them there, where my mother told me to.

This book is dedicated to helping you create a frame that you can build relationships around, that will support your unique vision of life, and add value to your life's experiences. The FRAME Formula is the answer to connecting and creating a little more magic in your relationships. It's a formula for building trust. This is also a formula for displaying your confidence and trust in your relationships and in the people you trust. Through the use of the FRAME Formula you will be able to integrate the many different types of frames in your relationships. You will have a FRAME for building around and strengthening from within as well as a FRAME that adds value and showcase your hard work and love.

Our frame of reference is also called our point of view. So what is point of view? It is our personal priority for desired outcomes and values. It makes us who we are and what we want to do in this life. It frames our outlook and expectations.

A frame of reference is important because it helps us know where we came from. It allows us to relate to and analyze the world around us. This in turn contributes to the decisions we make and helps us to make sense of what is happening around us. It forms our expectations. One thing we often don't realize is that our FRAMEs are exchangeable. We can choose to change them, embellish them, or put them down and pick up another.

A FRAME is always there. Always. It is always there whether or not we use it intentionally. It is always underlying and surrounding the way we interact with ourselves and the world around us. This is what people mean when they invite us to "walk in their shoes." What they are really asking is for us to see it from their point of view, or look through their FRAME. Everyone wants us to do this but no one has ever taught us how before. When you have completed reading this book, you will be one of the lucky ones who know.

At the end of each chapter there is a "POP Steps" section. This is where you find the Pulled Out for Practice pieces for each level in the FRAME Formula.

F: FREEDOM TO SPEAK

It was a blessing that the only television in the house was not on. Every other possible thing that could make noise was doing so. Kids were asking for help with homework, playing games together, and practicing their instruments. Water was running in the kitchen as dinner dishes were getting washed. Other than the noise, everything was in order and happy.

I had become accustomed to the insanity of it all until my phone received a text message "Ah. Evening jazz with Dallas." It was from a neighbor across the street and three houses away up the hill. That was my first hint that there was an issue with our volume. Then I took the garbage from the kitchen to the can outside. When I closed the door it merely muffled the sounds. Our family could be heard from the street and beyond. And it wasn't just the trumpet. The level of noise was atrocious. The neighbors up the hill could easily hear, and there were no secrets to be had when everyone was trying to talk louder than the others so they could be heard.

I stood at the curb and listened. They were happy sounds, but they were out of control. A couple was taking a walk on the other side of the street. They looked towards our house and whispered to each other, then glanced at our house again. It was like they were trying to keep a secret about what they heard emanating from our walls. As I watched them round the corner I thought, "This is ridiculous. We don't have to be this loud. Why are we? How do I change it to be ... normal? Or at least confined to our house and not filling the entire neighborhood?"

The answer came to me quickly. Structure and order. We had a little, but it wasn't enough to provide a feeling of safety and freedom to speak. The kids didn't feel like they could have a turn to talk. And if they talked, they didn't feel like what they said could be heard. Something had to be done.

Here's what we did. It's called the FRAME Formula. Just like Maslow's Hierarchy of Needs suggests that lower levels support the upper levels, the FRAME Formula builds on itself and supports the upper levels. Maslow's Hierarchy, in simplest form, states that there are five levels of human needs. Each level is supported by the previous level. For example, the middle level is belonging. While it is not impossible for someone to feel like they belong when the levels below—order, safety, and base need—are not present, the feeling of belonging is easier and more sustainable when they are fulfilled, or in the process of being fulfilled. When the basic needs of shelter and food are not met it is difficult to create order and safety or belonging.

The FRAME Formula is the Hierarchy of Needs for communication. The base level, or foundation, that supports the rest of communication, is freedom to speak. If someone does not feel as though they have the freedom to speak, they won't. If it was a goal to have them cooperate in house chores it is not impossible, but it is easier to get compliance when the base need of freedom to speak is fulfilled.

The diagram below illustrates and outlines the levels of The FRAME Formula.

Every
One
Wins

Make it
Meaningful

Accountability
and Action

Respect and Honor

Freedom to Speak

Meowing Ice Cream

My oldest son, Stephen, was four years old. He had always been a quiet child, more observant and cautious than his peers. I enjoyed his careful attention to details. I found it adorable and wished I could focus on one thing at a time as long as he did. Since he was quite large for his age it never crossed my mind that there was anything wrong with him. He was a brilliant, careful observer and would talk and interact when he wanted to later.

When he was only 8 months old and people asked when he was going to start walking. I thought they were crazy. He was not delayed. He only appeared slower because he was advanced in size. When the same people started asking when he was going to start talking, I felt the same. He just looks like he should talk more. He will.

It was during the trauma of the quadruplets being born and coming home from the hospital one at a time when I realized his cute quirks were really symptoms and signs of autism. Like most people, the stress accentuated his symptoms. He shut down and stopped talking altogether. We still did not seek a diagnosis, believing that his symptoms were resulting from the stresses of his young life. I didn't worry about what would later be diagnosed as high functioning autism, sometimes called Asperger's Syndrome. At his regular check-up the pediatrician recommended I spend more time with him, laughed, and wished me luck.

One day, I got a couple of sitters for the other kids and took Stephen to the grocery store. My goal was to have him feel and believe that he was worth listening to and that I valued his opinions. It didn't exactly work the way I had planned. When I asked, "Which flavor of cereal would you like?" he answered, "MEOW!" and pointed at the flavor he wanted. I thought cereal wasn't a powerful enough choice to use a word for. I tried ice cream next. It was the same. Through the entire shopping trip, I asked which one for everything we could choose. And everything I asked had the exact same answer: "Meow!" and a pointed little finger.

We finished the shopping and went home. I was at a loss for what to do next. Could there really be something wrong with Stephen? What was I doing wrong as his mother?

The image of Maslow's Hierarchy of Needs that I had recently studied in my college class came to mind. This was a concept that basically stated levels of goals and abilities are supported by things in lower levels. I took to studying it again with Stephen in mind. I couldn't believe what I found.

The lower levels are basic needs, like food and water, which support security.

Then security supports the ability for socially reaching out and building belonging. That's where it hit me. Talking was a social level goal. He didn't feel like he belonged enough to talk. I was expecting Stephen to speak with people while he was too scared to talk. He didn't have enough structure and safety around him to support this level of a goal.

I asked myself, "What is missing? What can I do to support Stephen in feeling safe?"

When I discovered what Stephen needed to feel safe it didn't seem related to his not talking at first, but I followed the impression that came to my mind. Even if it didn't seem related it was a real situation that could use some improvement.

We had been living in survival mode so much for so long that the little structure that I saw in our life was not seen by Stephen. He had a different point of view than I did. His frame of reference was complete chaos. While I knew he was going to be fed something by someone every day, he did not. He was wondering where he was going to be and who he was going to be with every day. He did not know what he was having for dinner or when he was having dinner. In his eyes, he couldn't rely on getting dinner. He didn't feel safe in this base level need.

Of course, the adults around were always taking care of him. He was never left without food. But because we had so much help—and chaos because of the four babies—he and his two-year-old brother Dallas were being looked after by different people each day. The structure was not stable.

There were other components to this instability. I would forget what time it was and we would often eat something at bedtime instead of dinner time. I rarely had a plan for dinner myself. If they were home with me for dinner it was whatever could be found. Breakfast came too early for me between changing diapers and washing bottles.

I didn't have a plan. There was always something to eat, but it was never planned or scheduled. When I discovered this, I quickly wrote down a few ideas:

- Breakfast: Cereal
- Lunch: Sandwiches
- Dinner: Spaghetti. Dinner is at 6:00PM

It took me about ten seconds to write it down, two more to post it and maybe a whole minute to show Stephen. He nodded and went on his way. I was amazed at how this simple moment of planning changed the day. We repeated this the next day. The meals were not extravagant by any means. Cooking the food didn't take any more time than it had before. The only difference was that I had made a plan. This was a life changing realization.

Having a plan eased my mind--and Stephen's—in ways that I could never have expected. By the third day, Stephen was comfortable and confident. He interacted with the other kids differently and spoke much more often. He was feeling safe. He knew he would have food. That's level one.

The next level involves structure and order, which was fulfilled by posting the plan. Creating that order allowed him to focus on the next level up, which is belonging. And this is where we were striving for the accomplishment of talking with other people.

By small and simple things, great things are brought to pass. We moved his frame of reference from stress and anxiety to confidence and peace by taking a few minutes to ponder and find his base needs. Then we invested less than five minutes a day to fill his needs.

The Uncomfortable Pause

Taking time out for figuring out what Stephen needed was a challenge. It was against all my logic at the time to stop caring for the kids as a whole and focus energy on just one of them. I worried I would be neglecting the other needs of the family. I worried that it was selfish of me to take a pause to catch my breath. I worried that if I wasn't there somehow life would end when I blinked. None of that was true. Taking a pause was a critical step for our family to move forward and progress. The entire family, and especially me as the mother, was blessed by the pause.

The world is currently moving so fast we don't know what to do with ourselves when there is even a half-second pause. It becomes uncomfortable and the space fills with uncertainty, worry, and judgments for the people we are with and ourselves.

So many times, I have seen teachers skip over the vitally important pause. It's a moment for thinking and processing our thoughts. We have been told over the years to think before we speak but we don't allow the time for it. We are expected to speak right away. I have learned that some people think out loud and process by speaking, and others cannot speak until they have had sufficient time to process and be sure they are saying the "right" thing.

My second son, Dallas, is so much like his mother (that's me.) He and I both speak out loud in order to process. Some people literally do need to hear themselves talk, just to hear it. Things don't make sense when they are stuck in my head. I will often warn the people around me that I am just thinking out loud and nothing that I say is real unless it sounds good.

Some people, like Stephen, don't want to offend or embarrass others- -or even themselves—by thinking out loud. For someone like Stephen, the language takes a long, detoured route to get to the lips and actually be spoken. Just because someone is quiet is no reason to assume they are not thinking. They are probably thinking much more than you expect.

Many times the thoughts will take a path of their own and Stephen needs to be reminded that I have not heard his answer yet. Sometimes he has been so deep in his thoughts and processing his words that he thought he did say something out loud. But he only thought about saying it.

When I have been waiting for a response for a long break, I choose to remind the person I am talking with that I am listening as opposed to waiting for their response. When they are reminded I am waiting, it causes rushed and often hurt feelings. The message sent is that they are not worth waiting for. It's the opposite effect desired for the magical pause. When the words are "I am listening" instead of "I am waiting" the message sent is, "I want to hear what you have to say."

In music a rest is needed to take a breath. It brings life and excitement to the song. The mistake is to think that taking a break is letting something, like a conversation, die. It doesn't kill it unless you decide it does. A pause is taking a break, waiting, resting. It's not the end.

Stephen at Junior High

The transition from elementary school to junior high was a difficult one for Stephen. He was leaving all he knew behind. He went from one teacher and one class to seven classes with seven different teachers. He went from playing outside during recess breaks to crowded halls with strangers looking for the next classroom, hoping to not be lost, hoping to not bump into a bully by accident, and hoping to be on time. Just thinking about it stresses me out. I can only imagine how he felt about it. Stress has shown to be an instigator of the shut down for my son and it showed here as well. With his autistic diagnosis he was given an Individualized Education Plan (IEP). This was a legally binding document stating that said he had some special things that needed to be known and adhered to by the school staff. He had a teacher that was to oversee the implementation of this plan and care for him in a protective way. She was called his "file holder" and any questions or issues were to go through her, like the middle man for organizing all the teachers in behalf of his needs. Sounds like a good idea, right?

One day Stephen came home all upset and stressed out even more than usual. He was being followed from class to class by a lady that kept trying to talk to him. He didn't want to talk to this stranger. He said she was stalking him. I had no idea what he could be referring to. His IEP didn't mention anything about having anyone with him all the time, though I knew it was an option for other people.

We went to the school to meet with his file holder. Her classroom was gray and dismal, but the whole school had that kind of feeling. Her smile made it feel bright enough in her room.

Then she started talking and any sort of imagined brightness quickly diminished.

I told her of the stalker: "Someone's following him around everywhere and he doesn't know who she is."

"He does too know who she is. She is with him every day all day long! Of course he knows her. She's his personal aide!"

Her look of shock could only be outdone by my own. We had specifically mentioned in his IEP that he did not need an aide. I tried to contain my anger, expecting, of course, that it was just a misunderstanding. I doubted myself first. There must be something happening at school that I was not aware of. They should have his best interest at heart. I told myself to figure out who it was and what was happening before jumping to any conclusions. The most important thing for understanding right now was who is following my son and why doesn't he know who they are.

I asked, "Did you tell him about her? Did you introduce them?"
What she said next threw me for a loop.
"No. He wouldn't talk to me if I tried!"
Talk about jumping to conclusions!

The issue with the aide was resolved but the expectations of who my son was and what was expected of him was not. His file holder had decided before meeting him that his paper said he had autism and that meant not talking. Her frame of reference was imposed on my son without getting to know him as an individual. This may be true for many autistic people, but it was not true for Stephen. My son would talk to you if you wanted to hear what he had to say, if he felt safe, and if you gave him the time for him to process the language to the point of leaving his lips. And even if he didn't talk, I also firmly believe that a person still can communicate who they are and what they need in many other ways.

We switched schools and went somewhere they did not have the same expectations. Within a few months his new teachers were absolutely loving Stephen. One of them told me that if all of her students were like Stephen, she would live in heaven. He was obviously her favorite student, out of all of her hundreds of students. This teacher asked if he had any siblings that she could have in her classes in the future. She loved him. She showed that she cared about him. He felt safe to participate in class and express himself as needed. He loved being there and would stay after class every day to push all the chairs under the tables on his way out.

Stephen was still autistic, but when the teacher was able to take the extra time to pause and wait for his response instead of giving up and moving on, he gave her the desired results of opening up.

Pause for Safety

Maybe the person you want to connect with doesn't have a problem of not talking.

Maybe you have a person who can't seem to stop talking, like another of my sons, Brenden.

Brenden will talk, and talk, and talk, whether you are listening or not. If you are in the same room with him, he will be saying something. He probably talks to me when I am not there too, but I can't verify that. Brenden needs to share every detail about everything. Even if you don't respond, he will tell you anyway. If you let him go without interrupting him, he might just repeat himself in order to be sure it was said.

One day I was in the kitchen cooking dinner. Noodles were in the pot and I was stirring in the cheese. Brenden came in and started going on about a book he was reading. It was like he was reciting the book with added commentary. I was getting exasperated with his nonstop talking and the thought came to me that perhaps I could tell him that was enough. Perhaps I could tell him that I didn't care about that book, or his thoughts about it. My ears were just about ready to fall off. My day had been a bit rough and my patience was terribly thin.

I had a little conversation with myself in my head. I told myself, "No. Just give him a little more time. Your ears won't really fall off. You don't have anything to do but stand here and stir the pot. You can do that while he talks. Try to listen to what he is saying."

"That's great advice, if do say so myself. Thank you, self."

So I took a pause and tuned in to what he was saying a little more. I tried to really listen and see what he was so excited about.

It took about five seconds for his demeanor to change. Simply pausing and not interrupting or judging him provided him with a safe place to be himself, to be valued and appreciated. Brenden saw that he was in a safe place and that he could talk to me. He saw that I was listening. Suddenly he stopped reciting the book, looked at me, and took a deep breath. His lower lip trembled a bit when he said, "Mom. I have a problem. I need your help."

That was a brave, big, step for a ten-year-old. I am ever grateful that I listened to myself and took a pause for my relationship as his mother.

Give Permission

I remember a time when my kids were all riding with some friends in the back of our van. We were going to scout camp and everyone was really excited. I was listening intently to their conversations, trying to become part of the background and be forgotten so I could learn some secrets they have or something, like a ninja mother would.

There were seven boys and myself. All of them were contributing to the conversation in various ways, not necessarily taking turns but every one talking and excited. They all seemed to take a breath at the same time and literally less than three seconds passed before someone said out loud, "Awkward silence..." and they all started talking again. "I know!" "Right!" "Weird!"

And the trip was never quiet that long again.

Children need to have permission and to know when it is their turn. Who gets to go first and how long do they get to talk before it is someone else's turn?

We tried a few fun ways to know who was allowed to speak, like if you were holding the stuffed animal then you got to have a turn to talk. This led to more arguing and quarreling over who got to have the stuffed animal. Some of the kids were reluctant to give it up and everyone just yelled about it being their turn.

Today, we still have moments when we need reminding that it is someone else's turn. I often will pull out the timer and give a 30 second warning. Even then there are one or two kids that think they just need to talk anyway.

Pausing is also a great way to let others know they have permission to speak. We wait for someone to take a breath so we can contribute to the conversation and longer pauses may begin to feel uncomfortable and awkward until someone else starts talking. It's okay to have a moment of silence to let our thoughts settle down into a pattern that will make sense coming out of our mouths. Sometimes we need to think before we speak. It's not just a saying. It's a real thing that takes some time. Usually we feel like we have to respond right away because it feels awkward if we have silence for a few seconds. But it's simply allowing time to formulate what we want to say.

If you are a person like me, who processes their thoughts out loud, thinking before you speak will be a challenge. Depending on who the listening party is there are a few ways to think out loud and still think before you speak. You could preface the conversation by saying something like, "I'm going to listen to your side and then take a moment to myself to process before I answer." I like to preface my thinking out loud by stating to the people around me that I am thinking out loud. This might sound like a silly solution but the simple solutions are almost always the best ones.

When we don't feel free to speak, there is hesitation and doubt in sharing thoughts at all. If you find that you are not able to think before you speak, the pause in your case would be for the other participant in the conversation to pause and wait for you to finish processing. Invite them to wait while you process and then you will tell them the answer. At that point, you can say something to the effect of, "Ok, here's what I came up with", or, "what this means is…"

When I encounter a speaking-to-process person, like Brenden or Dallas, I will ask them if they are thinking out loud or if I should be paying close attention. They will often say I don't need to pay attention all the way yet. Then, when they find their thoughts ready to share, they say, "Okay Mom. Are you ready to listen?" Conversations become less judgmental and more enjoyable when the thought process is separated from the thoughts that are sharable.

When we have a one-on-one conversation it is natural to have longer pauses to think about our responses. When we want to get a response, it's okay to let the other person think about it or recognize that they are expected to fill that silence. In person communication is different than electronic communication. You can't pick an emoji out of the air in person. You can't click the "like" button in person. You have to take time to formulate how to say that emoji in words.

Giving permission means we don't interrupt. In my family we have a hard time with this one. I often interrupt my kids when they are talking about something irrelevant to getting the dishes clean or another end goal. I see this as a place I really need to improve and as I have made changes it has been like magic. There's a certain power in a conversation when I can say to my teenager, "I listened to you without interrupting. Now, please, hear me out."

POP Steps

One of the key factors for helping children to have the safety and freedom to speak is validating their feelings, thoughts, and opinions. A great way to do this is to take a pause.

Pausing is a part of creating freedom to speak. It works for both the "non-talkers" and the "can't stop talking" people. It works like magic. Pausing is a way to show we respect who our children are. We respect them enough to take a few minutes to listen and learn about who they are, what they need, and how we can be part of it all.

At first I had to train myself to take a pause and really be patient. I would count for a few seconds to make sure I was really allowing them time to process and have a turn. For a talker like Brenden, I would count to ten, if he would wait that long. For Stephen, I would count much higher. I would often give him a full two minutes before reminding him that I was listening.

Then, when he got that reminder, he would let the words spill out.

Just like Maslow's Hierarchy of Needs, there is a hierarchy for nearly everything. The lower levels form a foundation that supports the higher-level goals. Freedom to speak is the base foundation level of the family communication hierarchy of needs. As we work up through the levels, we find a framework for structuring great communication and building a family-culture around. I call this framework The FRAME Formula.

First look at what goals you are working to achieve. Then ask, "What would support this achievement in the lower levels? What is missing? How can I provide that?"

This is identifying the base needs. Each individual will have individual needs that vary depending on the frame of reference, or point of view.

When the base needs are met there is a level of increased safety. Safety supports the growth of respect and honor.

NOTES:

NOTES:

R: RESPECT AND HONOR

What is this thing people call respect, and why is it so hard to find? One example of having respect is to obey when a request such as "clean your room" is made. If there is a good deal of respect there will be a conversation, or quick obedience. Many people say they have respect because their demands are always fulfilled immediately.

Obedience is not always out of respect. There are many reasons a person, especially a child, will obey without argument. Sometimes there is obedience because of fear. It may look like respect because there is little to no argument. It is not real respect if they are living in fear. Fear inspires resentment and secrecy. The word "fear" invokes cowering, hiding, and negative emotions. Respect, on the other hand, is a lifting energy. We look up in admiration when we respect. Admiration accompanies respect.

Take a hero for example. We look up to, admire, and respect heroes. A hero can come in any shape or form. If we were looking up to a "hero" figure, it is because of something awesome they did or a skill they possess and share. It is not because we fear them. We have respect for them.

I know someone, let's call him Joe, who had a favorite football team and respected that team so much that he was willing to do anything to defend them. When a fan of a different team, we will call Daniel, shared his opposing view, it was as if he had become an enemy. They were watching a football game on TV together, as friends. It was the first time they were watching football together and did not know they were rooting for the opposite team. Daniel's team gained a touchdown, much to the discouragement of Joe. Daniel cheered for the touchdown. Joe was so upset about it that he threw a penny at his new "enemy." The penny was the closest and most available weapon around. Daniel was shocked as the penny flew through the air and struck him between the eyes. Watching this made me think: Joe looked up to the team so much that he was willing to defend them physically. He had never met them before, yet he was willing to damage a relationship with a real person over a differing of opinions.

There was a young man named George who was looking forward to getting married. A few months before the wedding he was visiting his future in-laws in their home. His future brother-in-law, John, was in the corner reading a magazine while George, his bride-to-be Sally, and a few others in the family were having a conversation about feet.

Sally pointed out how her feet were wider than her brother's. George noticed his toes were longer and thinner than almost everyone else there. Sally's mom noted that her feet were dry and said did not care for the shape of her toes. She said, "My toes are ugly. I have ugly feet."

Being new to the family, George did not know what to say other than agree with her. As soon as he said, "Okay" there was a burst of energy flying into his face. It took a moment for George to realize it was John defending his mother. John's fist was next to George's chin as he threatened, "That's my mom you're talking about!"

George wisely apologized and promised to never agree with her about her feet being ugly again. John calmed down, and life went on. The point is that John had respect and honored his mother to the point of defending her, even if it was about something as silly as agreeing with her about her feet.

Honor cannot live in fear. Real respect is about looking up to and honoring a person. This kind of respect leads to increasing honor. We may not always remember what was said or what happened. We remember our feelings and how a person makes us feel, how a person creates a feeling of honor and respect. So, the question is, how do we get teenagers and kids to show us respect?

The answer is the Golden Rule. If you want it, give it. Treat others the way you want to be treated. You're probably thinking, "I've heard this before." Well, here's the next part that isn't talked about everywhere. The secret special sauce is: not expecting anything in return. Hope for it. Plan for it. But don't get upset if it takes longer than you want for it to come back to you. Remember, find a way to give a sincere compliment, regardless of whether you receive anything back in return. We are not nice to people because others are nice to us. We are nice to people because we are nice people.

It is up to us to define who we are. The people around us will believe us when they have enough evidence for it—when they trust us. We must trust first, or trust will be hard to find. Just like the Golden Rule, if we want to be trusted we must trust first. There may not be evidence for trustworthiness. Trust anyway. Then verify. Find evidence to support the trust. Seeking evidence before trusting is like condemning the other person. It's like saying they are guilty until proven innocent. Seeing the world in this negative way repels open communication.

An example of increasing respect and open communication is accepting personal greatness. Hiding our greatness makes everyone feel less, as if we didn't trust ourselves and who we are. It's dishonest. It lacks respect for self. It disgraces any honor that might be there. Respect means to accept the whole truth, even the awesome parts.

A common mistake related to refusal to acknowledge accomplishments is the belief that if you ignore your greatness then you are humble. The idea is to avoid the appearance of prideful bragging.

There is a difference between being prideful and being honest. I admit, there is a tricky balance there that many people will not be able to find. I stand by the truth anyway. Everyone has something they are good at. Everyone has some sort of gift that is theirs to embrace, grow, and share with the world. Your job, and mine, is to find that gift and let our kids know we see it. It's our job to give that sincere compliment in complete respect and to honor who they are.

Someone somewhere decided that it wasn't okay to brag about accomplishments because that would make other people feel less about themselves. I would like to disagree appropriately. In fact, I believe that the less we accept the truth about ourselves and the people around us, the less valuable and worthy everyone feels.

The Gifted Octopus

My second born son, Dallas, is brilliant. No way around it. He just is. When he was young he showed me one of his math tests that was 100% and I praised him. "You must be one of the smartest kids in your class!" Even though he earned a high score and it was true that he was very good at math, he didn't like it. "You can't say I'm good at something, Mom!" He explained how at school they were taught not to brag about getting good grades because bragging makes people feel bad.

He was mad at me for giving him the compliment. As his mother, this both broke my heart while at the same time, it touched my heart that he would care about other people's feelings so much. This battle of heart's opposition was won by my broken heart and I called all the kids to a meeting for a learning moment.

Of course I want my children to be observant and care for others, but I also do not want them to be a doormat and not care about their own feelings. There is a balance to be had. We can't give what we do not have. If we do not care about ourselves, then we cannot fully care about others. Our discussion that day has turned into the octopus story.

The octopus is an incredible creature—brilliant as a creature who lives under the sea. They do not create or build cities. They do not learn to read or do math. However, they are brilliant in their own ways. It is well known that if you own an octopus, whether in a zoo or as a pet, you must cage it well, as they are masters of escape. There have been many examples of an octopus opening doors and removing lids from sealed jars. In fact, they recommend you give the octopus a challenge so it doesn't get too bored. Even though they don't study science the way humans do, the octopus knows and can accomplish everything it needs to live in its world under the sea. Respect and honor can be given for the octopus and its unique abilities.

Unlike an octopus, I do not have any knowledge of how to survive in the ocean. I would not do well there at all. Every living being or creature on planet earth has knowledge and gifts that are theirs alone. I do not complain that the octopus gets compliments for being a master at camouflage or escape. And it does not complain that I might get a compliment on my math skills.

My brother was excellent at skateboarding, welding, and fighting forest fires. Not me. I'm really good at organizing and making plans, like the time I planned to take the Christmas lights off the roof of our house. Then my brother came to rescue me when I couldn't figure out how to get back down. We have different strengths to help us work together.

We should be more than satisfied that we are good at something, because that is how we contribute to the world. If one of us is better at math and another is better at science, we can work together to evaluate and create solutions to world problems. We take our strengths and build on them together. My son, or anyone else who has been embarrassed because they were awesome at something, requires praise and acknowledgment for their accomplishments and talents. Acceptance of the awesomeness. Respect and honor. Not criticism for recognizing that they are good at something

Everyone has something that a sincere compliment can be given for—being there, smiling, and brushing their teeth well (I love it when my kids brush their teeth really well!). Whatever it is, find it and share a compliment for it. There are ways we contribute to the world, and it is good to be acknowledged for our contributions. Contributing to the world is a requirement for happiness in life.

Being different often comes with an expectation that there will be disagreements. While building in level two of the FRAME Formula, remember that respect and honor is about having differences, including differences in opinions. We are not expected to agree on everything. When we have disagreements there is an appropriate way to communicate respectfully.

Disagree Appropriately

My husband and I read a book that talked about teaching children to disagree appropriately. So we tried it. The first thing to do is to state that there is a disagreement. When stated as a request it opens minds to having a discussion rather than an argument.

"I would like to disagree appropriately." These are very big words to hear from a 4-year-old's mouth. But they work. Asking permission to disagree or stating in a respectful manner that you do not agree made our home a more peaceful place. Not that everything was rosy all the time, but we knew that if we had a disagreement, like, "I don't think I need to do my homework until after the movie is over," we could discuss it. When we have this line of communication open it allows for us to agree.

That's right. We needed to make being open to disagreement in order for us to agree. If there are only expectations and rules to break, there is no agency and cooperation. This is living in fear, not obeying out of respect and choice.

Expectations are great. They are even better when they are agreed upon by the people who expect and are expected of.

If I told my kids, "Clean your rooms! Clean your rooms! Clean your rooms!" and they just kept ignoring me, hoping they would get to be forgotten in the mix of life, I would eventually get grumpy and probably raise my voice at them. This is an example of there being an expectation without an agreement. On the other hand, if I said, "You need to clean your room. Now is the best time," and we had an agreement in place that they were allowed to disagree appropriately, they would have no problem responding, "Can I disagree appropriately?" They could then express their desire to wait until the movie was over, or the game they were playing was finished, before cleaning their room. We could have a conversation about the expectations and agree together on a plan.

My second son was so verbal—openly expressing his thoughts and feeling—that some people thought he was manipulative and controlling. According to some people, he was too opinionated for a child and trying to talk him through a situation was "wasting time." This was false. Later we learned he had oppositional defiance disorder. Showing respect and honoring him was the only way to teach him how to show respect for anyone else.

There is always value in taking time to communicate with a child. If they are acting out there is a reason, usually because they have a need that is not being met. When we were able to instill the phrase, "I would like to disagree appropriately" in his vocabulary, our home became much more kind.

My mom would laugh that I had all these little people walking around our knees using such big words. The younger generation is just younger. It doesn't mean they are not able to learn or know things. Everyone, even a young child, has a point of view and therefore an opinion that is unique to them.

If we are all looking at a tree some of us would see the leaves and others would see branches, or part of the trunk. It is all the tree, but if we were to each describe what we saw, the descriptions would not always match. When we are not able to see the other points of view, we become disconnected. Part of respecting is understanding and allowing other people to see differently.

Brenden: The Sun Rises and Sets

When we have trouble connecting with people, we often feel like there is a lack of respect. Gaining and holding respect is where the real magic begins

There is a friend of respect that goes with it everywhere. It is called gratitude. If there is no gratitude there is very little respect, and vice versa. Think of the person you want to have more respect with, both respect from and respect towards. Who is it that you want to connect with most? What's the current level of respect with them? On a scale of 1to10, what number does it score? Take note of it. Now, let's make a comparison. What is the level of your gratitude towards them? Do the respect and gratitude numbers match? I bet they are pretty close if not the same.

I know what you're thinking, because I have thought it, too. How can I gain respect from them when they are so_____? Fill in the blank here with your favorite adverb. Rude, full of themselves, weird, crazy, or simply—disrespectful.

This may not come easily, but it will create the results you've been dreaming of. The fastest, most effective way to build rapport and respect is to make a gratitude list about the person whose respect you want to gain. It doesn't have to be a difficult task. Decide it will be easy. Above all decide it is worthwhile to have this particular relationship. Know that just like practicing improves anything, finding things to be grateful about them for will get easier as you write out your list. Watch it grow.

Part of the magic of the gratitude list is to having it physically written down, not just in your head. When we can see it, it becomes more real. The more senses involved, the more real it becomes. Writing involves hearing and processing words in our mind, seeing them on paper, and actively and tangibly experiencing the process of finding gratitude. Three learning styles of visual, auditory, and kinesthetic are represented when writing.

When it's only in our head, it's easier for our brain to argue with us about whether it is true or not. Letting the gratitude live only in the same place as our imagination gives reasons to say it's just imaginary. The subconscious tries to tell us that it's a dream to have so many things to be grateful for in that person. After all, there's lots of evidence against our claims of gratitude—otherwise we would not be struggling with respect.

So we write down things about them that we admire, things they have done, experiences they have gone through that were hard but they did it anyway.

It may need to begin as simple as:

- I am grateful so and so gets out of bed every day (and if they don't get out of bed every day, maybe it's more like, I am glad they don't breathe the air I am trying to breathe.)
- I am glad they are not in my face every second.
- I am grateful they are contributing to my learning to be patient.

Find a real, sincere way that having them in your life contributes to good. Find things that you share. Maybe you are sharing the trial of patience together. Finding things in common is a key to gaining respect. The goal of respect is to share common ground.

It isn't always easy to find that true and sincere compliment. I remember one day in particular, my son Brenden was driving me crazy, as usual. I was exasperated and so relieved for the hour he was able to go to his computer class. I sat in the waiting room just breathing and trying to collect myself. I closed my eyes. I took in one more long deep breath, preparing to be with him for the rest of the day. My thoughts turned to ideas of how to avoid being in the same room with him for more than five minutes. Guilt began to sweep over me and I did not have an answer. He was a sweet, innocent five-year-old who couldn't really do anything malicious if he tried. He was simply more than I knew how to handle. When class was over, I felt impending doom weigh me down as the door opened and kids began finding their parents.

The gloom over me was brightened as Ms. Rose's radiance entered the room. She followed my son and brightly approached me.

"Doesn't the sun just rise and set with that boy!?!"

I was shocked and amazed that her experience with Brenden was so drastically different than mine was. She loved him and loved being with him. Not that I didn't love him, but I certainly was struggling to enjoy my time with him. She had a completely different point of view. She was able to see his needs and the reasoning behind his behavior. I took this miracle of enlightenment home with me, her words echoing in my mind: The sun rises and sets with my boy. The sun rises and sets with my boy.

I let her words sink into my skin and I started finding ways that maybe someone with a different point of view, like Ms. Rose, would see him for who he is. Whenever there is a better point of view, one that makes a more positive and happier world, I try to realign my point of view to match.

Taking her example of finding the needs and seeing where he was coming from changed my experiences with him forever. He didn't need to change who he was. I needed to change how I saw him. If I could find at least one thing about him to have gratitude for, I could build it to respect.

This is what I did for Brenden. I saw that he made someone else happy. I could appreciate that. You may need to stretch to find it, but as long as a person is human there is something somewhere within them to be grateful for. After I wrote down "He makes Ms. Rose smile" I peeled back more layers to find out why he made her smile. What was it about him that she loved? Could I love him for that too?

It didn't take long for me to change how I felt and it showed in how Brenden treated me in return. It started with gratitude.

POP Steps

Gratitude lists lead to sincere compliments. What about having something in common?

That's where the love lists come into play.

A love list is a list of things that you love. What does the other person love? Where does the list of things they love overlap with the list of things that you love? Search for common ground and you will find stability in your relationship. Knowing what they like and what you like, the differences and commonalities between you, is identifying the point of view. This helps you understand where they are coming from and reduces disagreements overall. More than that, though, is the ability to build on the differences, like building blocks that only work when the different parts work together.

Working and building on differences takes creativity and time. The possibilities are endless, as shown in Stephen's creation here. (Photo by author)

Working together and contributing in the smallest amounts are wonderful things to put on the gratitude list and give sincere compliments for. It sounds like this:

- Thank you for your help.
- Thank you for being here.
- Thank you for sharing your ideas with me.
- Thank you.

Having mutual respect and honor supports working together.

NOTES:

NOTES:

A: ACCOUNTABILITY AND ACTION

Step three in the FRAME Formula is taking accountability for actions, and actually taking some action. This is where trust is built and fortified. The best examples of trust can be found in our relationship to nature. We trust the sun to rise. We trust everything to work well together as long as nothing interrupts it. Remember the law that says a body in motion will stay in motion and a body at rest will stay at rest unless a force is applied to it?

The laws of nature are in effect for our family relationships as well. Consider, for example, the give-and-receive cycle, which is everywhere in nature. There's the water cycle where water falls as rain, gathers in lakes and puddles, then evaporates into the clouds waiting to rain again. There's the oxygen cycle, where animals and plants work symbiotically, helping one another as each exhales the product the other requires to inhale for life to continue.

With people, we naturally want to give back when we receive. Receiving turns into taking when there's no giving back. Unlike the Golden Rule, this is not specific to one area of life. When we give, we can receive in any area to keep the cycle in balance.

The Give and Receive Cycle

The ability to be counted on

Holding people accountable for their actions can save lives.

I lay in my bed, unable to participate in anything more than growing the quadruplets soon to be born. Even sitting up for too long would put the babies at risk of being born too early. Full of growing children, being waited on hand and foot, and waiting for people to serve me, I felt helpless. Not contributing to anything in the world, other than protecting the pregnancy. Taking. And waiting to take more. This disrupted the give-and-receive cycle. Or, it could be called the receive-and-give cycle.

Either way you look at it, I wasn't giving. This is when I found my darkest hours. I felt detached from my family and guilty for not being able to take care of my other kids the way I believed I should. I felt like a huge burden on the world, even though all the help was happy to volunteer and so many people offered their encouragements and words of amazement. They said I was an inspiration, but I did not believe them. My dark thoughts and feelings secretly crept from me and seeped into my boys. A few years later, one of them began having suicidal thoughts, believing himself to be a burden.

When my son was experiencing his darkest hours we found that contributing was a major factor of getting him out of the suicidal thoughts. Being of worth in the world is vital. When we allow our young ones to help in the house and take responsibility for themselves, it creates a feeling of worth that can be had in no other way. We must let them become contributors and encourage them beyond the time it takes them to learn how to work so they can have pride in their accomplishments. It allows them opportunity to be counted on when they are accountable.

Letting the people we interact with have their own feelings and ideas to contribute to a conversation is equally important. People who are susceptible to depression start slipping when they are not heard or their thoughts are not validated and respected. They pick up on this through body language and the tonality used during conversations even when the person displaying has not said that they disagree with their opinions. We often share what's really in our minds without speaking.

When we allow others to have their own opinions and let them take accountability for themselves, it frees our own spirits from carrying their burden. We release the resentment and judgment that weighs the relationship down. When the weight is released, we can lift others. When they are lifted they feel more valuable and the downward spiral of depression can be reversed in many cases.

Think of the word ACCOUNTABILITY. Sounds like the ability to be counted on, right?

And it is.

Trusting to Build Trust

Before someone can be held accountable, there needs to be an agreement about expectations and consequences. Agreeing on expectations is a step towards building trust.

It can take a leap of faith to let other people agree to the expectations we set for them. Let's think about it, though. Would you rather have someone lovingly remind you, or constantly nag you to get something done? That's the difference in agreements. The energy and feeling about it is very different when we are informed and contribute to the agreement made. It goes back to the level of respect and honor, choice and agency, versus living in fear and force. Building on that level in the FRAME Formula, when we allow our children to participate or take action, as in step 3 in the FRAME Formula, in making the agreements they have a part in, then they can be held accountable.

Of course, when they are younger they will make agreements differently than they will when they are teenagers. But remember, they are smarter and better able to learn and progress than most people give them credit for. Kids are amazing and often have better vision and clarity in possibilities than adults do.

Nagging is not loved by the giver any more than the ... can we call them "receiver"? It's not really received when love is not involved. Real love means that there is a real trust present.

Trust is built by giving opportunities to prove that trust.

When my second son, Dallas, was about four years old, I was trying to get him to comply with my request to do a task. It had been a long day with him "ignoring me" and I lost my temper. Exasperated I said, "I have told you over and over!" He looked at me as slyly said, "How many times have you asked me?"

I fell into his game. I responded, "A lot! I have told you at least five times!"

Without looking at me, Dallas said in a matter of fact way, "Oh. Hmm. I thought you were going to tell me 17 times." He turned and went on his merry way until I told him 17 times. I actually counted because I know he was counting. (I know—you're thinking "a four-year-old?" Yes. He is unique.) After asking seventeen times he was very happy to comply, just like a perfect little angel.

The number 17 was not special. Rather, making a demand was a way for him to have control over something when his life was full of chaos. (Remember those quadruplet baby siblings?) He needed to have some influence in his world so he could feel like what he said mattered. As parents we often believe we are the ones in charge and we are meant to control our children. Our job really is to teach them and help them learn to have control themselves.

Until I had communicated the way Dallas expected, he was not going to cooperate. As soon as I knew he was expecting seventeen times, my frustration could take a back seat while I worked it his way. Children don't want to be controlled. They require guidance and structure to learn and progress in their own way. Frustration is only present when our expectations, either as a parent or a child, are not being met. Showing more flexibility as a parent in how we communicate with our children is how we win. It doesn't always have to be our idea. We don't always have to be the one getting recognition for knowing everything. And we don't have to do it our way every time. There is more than one way to do nearly everything. If we keep the end result in mind then it is okay to communicate in the child's learning style until they are able to understand and learn in other ways. Learning multiple languages, or learning styles, takes time.

It is only frustrating when we try to make things happen OUR way. If we know what each child's learning style and expectations are, we can work together better. As they get older, it is reasonable to expect more cooperation between both learning expectations and cooperation from the beginning without being asked seventeen, or forty, times. We build to that point by starting where they are.

How do we build that trust and cooperation? One way is to comply with their expectations and follow through with what we say we are going to. If we are doing what is expected, we are reliable, and that leads to trust. This is the give and receive cycle. Giving is action and taking action on expectations that are agreed to by both parties. Trust is received as accountability.

When we are trusting in our expectations there is no blame to be had. If we have had an open and honest conversation, there is no reason to doubt what will really be done. When we are all agreeing instead of just expecting, then we can agree to be trustworthy without blame. When children are fully aware of the consequences and expectations that they have agreed to, there is no whining or blaming, just accepting the consequences discussed.

It's easier to forgive when we have agreed on the situation. It's more obvious when an apology is needed, and it is more readily available when it was previously discussed and understood. The actions and accountability are made clear and cooperation can happen.

Alarming Breakfasts

There was a time when our quads were around nine or ten years old and Dallas and Stephen were about 13 and 14 years old. We were waking our children and making them get ready for school every day. I would wake Stephen and Dallas, then I would go down to the other rooms and wake the quads: Lily, Evan, Brenden, and Marek. Five minutes later I would go down again and turn the lights on. Then a few minutes later, my husband would do the same. It would take a half hour, or more sometimes, to get everyone out of bed.

One day I had a miraculous thought. "I do not like this. Wouldn't it be great if they all woke themselves up, and I could spend this time making breakfast or something for myself?"

We bought alarms for each of them. I know it sounds so simple and to me it was the most annoying idea I had ever had, almost. Having six different alarms going off, other than my own, waiting for them to wake up and turn them off, was not my idea of a great way to wake up in the morning. But it was the most amazing thing!

The next morning I was awakened by the sound of someone in the kitchen. Not crazy alarms. My 10-year-old son, Evan, had set his alarm and actually gotten himself out of bed and started making breakfast. When he came to tell me it was almost ready, he had a smile on his face and friendliness in his voice. There was a sense of accountability and accomplishment that turned into an opportunity for him to serve me. I cannot even express how this small investment in alarm clocks and the willingness to allow the children their own consequences changed our lives.

This was age appropriate for our kids. It was actually probably a little past due for the older boys, but the point is that there are things that can be done to encourage accomplishments and taking personal action at any age. Obviously when they are younger it will require more involvement from parents. But I do personally know a sweet girl who is only one year old who is beginning to tell her mom when it is time to clean up her toys and then does it. I have taught many young children between the ages of 18 months and two years old to participate in clean up time. Some have been very good at organizing the toys and running to help.

Does Evan make breakfast every day? No. But there is still a weight lifted from my shoulders. Now, years later, he still comes to me often and asks what he can make for breakfast.

When we gave our kids their own alarm clocks, I had no idea how far that responsibility transfer would take them. They had been confidently letting me boss them around. I was consistently grumpy about their lack of cooperation and their apparent desire to make me tell them everything over and over.

Taking accountability for our actions and allowing others the same courtesy allows for a level of reliability. Letting my kids wake themselves up with their own alarm clocks gave the opportunity to learn whether we could count on them or not. Being reliable and responsible can only happen by taking accountability for our actions. It's a step towards being trustworthy.

Being trustworthy is a key factor in successful conversations and relationships. Did you know allowing others to have responsibility was so important? Just imagine what would happen if I did not allow my kids to have their own alarms. What if I was too annoyed by all the noise? What if I was too worried that they wouldn't get to where they needed to be on time? What if I was too worried that their time of learning how to be responsible was embarrassing and reflected poorly on me as a parent?

In my future vision I do not see them turning out as confident and contributing adults if I had not let them take care of themselves more. The same goes for cleaning their rooms and everything else. They can only grow when we give them the opportunity and allow them to be accountable. That means that when they don't do their laundry, they don't have clean clothes and that's on them. Not me. The trick is to get them to agree that wearing clean clothes is important enough to do their laundry. Of course this is based on age appropriate skills and consequences. Remember, the ultimate goal is to raise children who become contributing, self-sufficient adults.

Forgiveness

As we build trust and start being able to rely and count on each other, forgiveness starts being more important. Before, when there is not as much agency, there is less chance to offend and make mistakes. When trust is broken, hearts often get broken.

Forgiveness hinges on point of view and understanding. It is rare that a person, especially a child, would intentionally break trust and hurt your heart because people are always good at the core. If we understand where they are coming from and what their intentions were, then it is easier to forgive.

I held onto negative emotions regarding my children for a time. Of course, I didn't tell them verbally, but the feelings were there anyway. It did not help anything at all. I blamed them for things that were out of their control or for things that I put on myself, like waking them up in the morning. Looking back, I laugh at how ridiculous I was. Until I was able to let go and forgive, our relationships were a strain on my soul. Being a better mother requires letting go of whatever negative emotions we put on our children. However, the biggest forgiveness was for myself. I had to agree that I could have done things better. It was not my kids' fault. I made choices and actions that were not the best for us as a family.

As soon as I decided that I was a contributor, I was able to have the power to change it. If we are blaming others we never get to take control and move forward. Being accountable allows us to take actions, to make choices, to think of options and create a path forward. Being able to create a path forward is critical in lasting relationships.

Level "A" in the FRAME Formula is what holds relationships together. This is where trust is built and strengthened. If there is no trust, the experiences together mean very little. No one wins. Every effort to make meaningful experiences and memories crumbles without trust. The respect and honor won't last if actions are not taken to strengthen the respect. Taking action and accountability for the actions is critical.

Sometimes this is easier to see in an unrelated story, so I have one to share with you.

My hungry belly growled as I stepped up to the fast food counter and placed my order. It had been several months since I had treated myself to a meal out and I was eagerly salivating before I requested my sandwich with extra lettuce and extra tomato. The kids were used to me ordering extra lettuce and tomato. It didn't faze them.

When my lunch arrived I noticed the missing extras right away. They made it wrong. I stared at my naked sandwich for a short moment before I stood. My son begged me not to make a scene. "Please don't, Mom."

I went back anyway. I had decided I wanted extras, and I had asked for and paid for the extras. It was all right for me to receive the extras. There was an agreement made between myself and the food place. I had done my part. I needed to allow them to do their part. So, I walked to the counter and told them what had happened. They apologized and gave me the extras. All was well. There was no blame or excuses and life was great. I thanked them and enjoyed a great sandwich. And I did not make a scene.

Another time and another place, I had ordered my lunch online ahead of time. I arrived a few minutes earlier than I expected. My lunch was not ready so the girl behind the counter gave me a free drink while I waited. I took it gratefully and thought how wonderful it was that they were so thoughtful. When I went to receive my food they apologized. That's where it should have ended. I was happy. They had done everything right.

But it did not end there. The restaurant staff continued to make excuses and reasons, taking my time and making me not only grumpy, but also a feeling of belittling came over me. It made me feel like I didn't matter. I wasn't a big enough order to take priority and they just didn't care about me. It did not matter why my food was not made yet. The truth is that I was early and didn't expect it to be ready yet. When they explained that they had lost my order it changed my feelings. When they continued and blamed it on a big order coming in, I felt like my order was not important to them, which led right into "I am not important to this business." This in turn led me to think, "I will not come back because they do not care about me and they are too busy to take care of me. I am hurting them by giving them more than they can handle."

See how the need for explaining and blaming hurts the people involved? At first I was just happy. All was well. I didn't mind waiting and I was actually impressed with their service, giving me a drink while I waited. But they had to keep talking. Let's be like the first example. Just say, "Yup. That is a mistake. I will fix it. Thank you." (Remember gratitude: "Thank you for bringing it to my attention and allowing me to do my part of the agreement.")

Yet, our first response for our children is often asking them why they did something. "Why"' only matters in the aftermath looking back to hopefully avoid making the same mistakes in the future. The question needs to change from "Why did that happen?" to "What can be done about it?" "Why" questions are blaming, while "What can be done" questions are action-taking and accountability-building.

POP Steps

Everything we want for our children—happiness, cooperation, belonging, confidence, communication, motivation, consistent personal improvement—can be accomplished through taking action and being accountable.

The power to change and improve is harbored within the accountability and responsibility taken for actions. Accepting and agreeing to a plan with consequences is empowering. It builds trust and confidence.

Accomplishment journals are used to further capture and enhance the progress and confidence. These journals can take any variety of forms from collecting pictures to writing out in a journal daily what was accomplished. I have a template we use in our family to help us stay on task. The kids can use it to check off goals for the day as they complete them. The template includes space for the vital gratitude and accomplishment counting, allowing it to track goals and progress all in one place. You can download a PDF copy of the accomplishment journal template at https://taggarttrainings.com/bonus/your-frame-formula-accomplishment-journal-template/

The biggest opposition I hear to using a journal is probably that it takes too much time, but it only takes a few seconds to choose and document a few things you are grateful for, and a few more seconds to capture your accomplishments each day. The rewards for tracking are beyond description. They are so worth the few seconds it takes! It's even better than getting breakfast made for you when you give the kids their own alarms.

The Accountability Template

DATE: _____

The emotion I chose to live in today is_____

I am thankful for $\left(\text{AM}\right)$ _____

$\left(\text{PM}\right)$_____

My Goal is _____

I want to achieve this goal because _____

_____

_____

The action steps I took toward achieving my goals today are _____

_____

_____

My action steps for tomorrow are _____

_____

_____

Today I learned _____

_____

The book I am reading right now is: _____

Today I did the following things

Listened to music	Made my bed	Washed laundry	Folded laundry	Put laundry away	Showered
Exercised	Washed my face	Brushed teeth 2x	Made Music	Vision board	Said declarations
Flossed my teeth	Was on time	Did homework	Gave compliment	Drank water	Took vitamins
Smiled	tidied up	Gave a hug	Acted Responsibly	Played	Daydreamed

NOTES:

NOTES:

M: MAKING IT MEANINGFUL

When the alarms were used my "good mornings" became really good instead of a chore. The call of "good morning!" had new meaning. We are entering the next level of the FRAME Formula—M: Making it meaningful. When I say "it" I mean your interactions and experiences with your children. By "meaningful" I mean that the time spent and experiences shared mean something more than an obligation. It's enjoyable and intentional.

Making it meaningful is the most important step of all. All of the other levels must be in order before you can really know if you are successful in making your interactions with your children meaningful or not.

If interactions are not meaningful, they mean nothing. Making experiences meaningful hinges on time—spending time to grow and strengthen the trust we have for each other. How we spend time and what we do with what we have learned makes all the difference in meaningfulness.

A Snuggle Trick

My second son, Dallas, reacted completely differently than Stephen to the trauma of having four new siblings added to the family. With his mother on bed rest and new people in our home helping every day, he went into a deep depression. He would verbally attack people nearby and express his frustration fully. Not being around much of this kind of emotional expression to learn by example, he would make up his own insults, like "You're just a flush down the toilet!" Dallas was full of anger and resentment as well as having lost his personal sense of worth.

At the beginning of this, I was advised again to spend more time with him. It seemed like the number one thing to help any of our children with whatever they needed was always to spend more time with them. The instructions were: Give them more attention.

Have you ever felt smothered by someone? It's like there's a heaviness weighing down on your shoulders. There's an urgency to get away, like a fire is coming at you. The fire demands all your attention, and the smoldering smoke begins to affect the whole family and your ability to survive. This is where I was when the doctor said, "Give him more attention." Then he laughed and added, "Good luck."

Dallas was clingy and mopey, constantly asking for a "snuggle." In my mind I thought I could not spend all day snuggling one kid. He was clingy to the point that I almost wanted to push him away so that I could breathe.

Being reminded that the most important ingredient in a relationship is time, I found a way to give him what he needed. At first I thought it was not going to be enough. I didn't think it was going to work, but I did it anyway. I set the timer for five minutes, just five measly minutes. That's all I could spare to devote 100% of my attention to Dallas.

I asked him what he wanted to do for his time. This was his to choose what he wanted to do with. Anything he wanted. Anything at all. He was in charge.

I looked into his bright blue eyes and heard his precious voice say, "Snuggle?"

A snuggle. He wanted to snuggle, and that is all. I should have seen it coming. We sat on the couch together, he nestled his head into my shoulder and we snuggled.

Two minutes passed and he had been satisfied.

"Mom, can I go play now?"

"No. Your five minutes are not up yet. Would you like to do something else?"

We ended up reading a book together, and he was happy enough that he didn't ask for attention for the rest of the day. The whole day!

This was so effective I set up "rotation stations" to rotate each child's turn for exclusive attention. After seeing it work for a few days, even though they were just infants, they all understood that they would get uninterrupted, full attention if they would patiently wait their turn. I felt some order settle into the crazy life and I was able then to add myself into the undivided attention rotations. Giving myself personal attention is the best investment I ever made.

Here's how the rotations support the entire FRAME Formula.

Setting up a routine and a schedule of expected attention provides a feeling of safety. When we feel safe, we feel free. Freedom can only be had when there is safety. That's step one: create safety.

The rotations provided a way for getting to know their individual needs and increase respect and honor. Step two achieved.

And, as we kept on the schedule while our children grew, we added to the rotations. There were times allotted for playing with a sibling, cleaning and doing chores, time with mom, time for playing their instruments, and more. It is a tool for holding us all accountable and knowing what agreements we have made. That's step three in the FRAME Formula.

As we had other kids come to play or when I tended kids for friends, we added them to the rotations. One summer day we had ten kids with ten things to do set up for a rotation. We came up with ten activities including LEGO® time, art time, ride bikes time, reading time, and so much more. It was the most organized and happy playtime we had ever experienced with our friends. They knew when snack time was and who they were going to build something with. This really made it meaningful. Step 4 accomplished.

The rotation stations is by far my favorite tool for building trust and spending quality time together. It walks right up every level of the Hierarchy of Needs and The FRAME Formula, starting with belonging and on to self-actualization, which is feeling so great you have to share with others. You get to the top of the levels and turn around to serve those around you. This final step is where everyone wins.

Having a plan is fundamental in increasing your abilities to serve. The rotation stations provide a plan that has allowed me to help my friends by tending ten young children in my home, all at once for an entire day, with joy. If I didn't have a plan I might have pulled my hair out.

I have been asked about teaching kids to be charitable and compassionate. The rotation stations definitely contribute to the kids' learning compassion by taking turns. They contribute their ideas and desires to put in the schedule and allow others to put their ideas in as well. It provides an opportunity to see other points of view and experience new activities.

I Need a PPI!

As part of the rotations we set up, we have weekly meetings with each of our kids individually. We call it having a PPI, or a Personal Parent Interview. This was separate from the rotation stations, but just as important in our family culture. We would set a time, typically each Sunday afternoon, and then tell the children who would get their turn first. Then we would have "free time" for everyone else.

We choose a place to have our meetings with the kids, close the door, and settle in. Often it is in our bedroom, sometimes it is in the office. Once in a while it will be in the child's room. There is always a door to close. Most of the time we bring a treat to share, like a lollipop or a cookie.

Our kids look forward to these meetings even as teenagers. It has set the expectation that we expect them to talk to us. We expect to know what they are up to, what they are thinking and feeling about different areas of their lives, and we expect to be able to support them in achieving their goals.

We have a list of topics we discuss that has evolved over the years as needed. When they were little we would ask them about homework and if they were getting along with their siblings well. This led us to change which of our kids were sharing a room at the time. We would not have known about the need if we didn't have a set time to address each individual's feelings.

Now that they are teenagers we ask about their friends and if they are interested in going to prom or not. Employment and transportation are big topics now.

PPIs are a time to learn about the individual. For some, like Dallas, we just sit down and start listening. He doesn't need any prompting to get a conversation going. Evan, on the other hand, is always quick to return the questions. He starts us off by asking how we, as his parents, are doing. We have modeled how to have a conversation, how to ask questions, and how to care about other people through the PPI system.

Stephen, however, needs questions to answer. One aspect of his Asperger's Syndrome is that he has so much to say floating around in his head that he doesn't know where to start unless we guide him to it. He has progressed so much that I often forget that he is different. He feels safe enough to talk most of the time at home, and maybe I am just so used to his quirks that they don't bother me. He will go about being himself. Then, if we have not had a PPI as scheduled, he will get so worked up about his internal struggles and feelings that he screams out, "Mom! I need a PPI!"

One day in particular he was extra worked up. I could tell because he was pacing and fidgeting his fingers. I said, "Hi Stephen. You okay?" He responded, "MOM! I need a PPI!" and started directly for the office. I followed him and closed the door behind me. Stephen knew how to get his needs addressed. He knew he could call for a meeting with me and he knew he would be heard and listened to. He knew I was there to help him. Many times we have talked with our kids during their PPIs about how we are there for them. We are on their team and we want them to win.

Stephen knew this was a safe place and he can reach out for help when he needs it. I watched him as he paced back and forth for a while, wondering what was in his head, waiting for him to find his words. When he couldn't handle it any longer, he shouted, "Ask me questions!"

I asked, "Is this about school? Your grades? A teacher? A friend? A girl?"

He shook his head until I hit the right topic and he flooded me with his words and concerns. Thirty minutes later he was calm and confident with a plan for what to do.

It takes time to make it meaningful. Asking for a PPI in our family means there is an urgent matter that needs immediate attention. It also is a set appointment in our schedules. Most of the time they are not very long, but on occasion we give the time necessary. It's an expectation. Clear expectations further build trust.

POP Steps

You are going to have a PPI. Choose where and when you will have it. If the child is old enough to have a schedule of their own, talk with them about when is a good time for you to meet together. If they are younger, let them know ahead of time that you will be having a meeting on your schedule. That way they can plan for it. The anticipation and expectation of having personal time with their parent will influence their behavior leading up to the PPI.

Once you have set the time and place, follow through with it. This is the most important part of all. Hold yourself accountable and show up. Build another layer of trust.

You can use the PPI Map at the end of this chapter as a guide for what to discuss in the PPI.

You can make the PPI part of your rotation stations. Set the timer as needed and keep on it. If there is a topic that needs more in-depth conversation that comes up in the PPI, schedule more time for it. Make it as soon as possible, but honor the schedule set for the other kids (if you have more than one child). Say something like, "I want to talk about this more. Let's add another ten minutes after the rotations are done." Wanting instead of needing shows that you care about them and desire to have the conversation. Needing to talk implies that there is obligation, which there very well may be. But we want to have the conversation even if we need to. When we say we want to talk it translates to the subconscious as we want to be with them—that they are wanted and not just an obligation. Taking this step builds trust and respect for the other kids in the family as well as gives you a little extra time to think of what to say, get your emotions in check, and fully be present when serious topics come up.

The PPI Map is a form you can use as a guide for your first few PPI meetings. As you progress and practice you will know what your children need to discuss. Even though I don't always use this PPI Map, I still like to take notes of our conversations so I can refer back to them and remember what needed to be addressed. Often if they seem happy and all is well, a topic that was important before can miss a follow up. When things are going well and a follow up might be considered frivolous and unnecessary, it is still helpful in building the respect and honor. It shows that you care about them when things are followed up on. It gives opportunity to celebrate together. Most of the time I have things that I need to do in order to support them that I need to have documented. Did I pay for club fees—buy wrestling shoes—sign that doctor's note—ask Grandma if we left a blanket there—yet? Most importantly, we keep record of the agreements we make. The rewards and promises are written down so we are all able to see exactly what is agreed on. It holds both sides accountable. For example, this week Brenden was asking if I had ordered his reward from Amazon. My notes from the PPI let me know whether I had done it.

Your Personal Parent Interview Map

The PPI Map is a form you can use to cover all the bases in conversations. You can download a copy at https://taggarttrainings.com/bonus/the-frame-formula-ppi-map/

The PPI Map

In every PPI visit, cover each level of needs.

- Base needs – time, food, health.
- Safety- issues with bullies or
- Belonging – friendships and clubs
- Goals and achievements – school grades and future ideas or wishes
- Influence/service – might show up when asking about friends and goals. Where's the give back?

Take notes and record for easy follow up each week.

- Hi. How are you? What's going on in your world?
- What's happening at school?
- Who have you been sitting with at lunch? Are you eating all your lunch?
- Tell me about recess/extracurricular activities – like piano lessons or scouts, sports or whatever they are into. List them out and ask about each activity/friends involved in each one.
- How are your interactions with your siblings lately? Are you becoming best friends?
- Is there anything you are struggling with?
- What goals are you working on? (Could be anything from passing a class at school, to getting a brother to not poke them, to growing their hair out)
- What can I do to help support you?
- What else would you like to talk about today?

Also go over any scheduling or calendar needs for the week, including an assigned chore if that is part of your family culture. Assigning chores is a way to give back and serve.

NOTES:

NOTES:

E: EVERYONE WINS

My daughter, Lily, oldest of the quads, is very different from my boys. Practically everything she is—or does—is unique. We said for a while it was because she was a girl, but it wasn't really. One aspect in particular was especially challenging because of her difference in learning.

All five of my boys could read before they were out of kindergarten. Most of them could read before starting school. As the quads were entering second grade, Lily could not tell the difference between a number 5 and the letter S. That is common. But she also could not tell if the S was a 2. She could not read. And she knew she was different.

That Christmas she said, "I want to ask Santa Claus to make me smarter for Christmas."

It broke my heart to tell her Santa doesn't work that way! In the following months Lily did not progress at the same rate the rest of the first graders did. She started being "sick" all the time, having stomach pains and missing school.

I noticed a pattern in her behavior. She was sick on days there was school and not on other days. When she was sick and stayed home from school, she healed miraculously as soon as she was told she could stay home. She was having anxiety about not being good enough, to the point of literally making herself sick.

She moaned in her bed one morning, holding her belly with tears in her eyes. I could see the worry all over her face. I had spoken with her teacher about the situation and, as had often happened in the past, when I told educators that I thought Lily needed more of something, her teacher told me to stop comparing her to the boys. It was implied that I was creating this problem for her, and that she was normal while the boys were weirdly advanced in their learning.

It was especially easy for Lily to compare herself to her brothers. Although they were not in the same classroom, they were in the same grade. She didn't need anyone else doing the comparing for her. There is a point where a person is smart enough to know themselves. We were coming to the fork in the road where we were going to make a decision, with or without the school's opinion.

On report card day they all stood in the front room, the sunshine bouncing off the walls around them, and each of them with giant smiles on their faces. Marek took off his jacket and revealed a big sticker on his shirt. The sticker read, "Ask me about my math test." So I did. His smile grew even bigger as he announced he got 100% on his math test. We all congratulated him with hugs and high fives. Then we began reading report cards. Lily was first—she had received all A's. A perfect score for a first grader. I thought how odd it was but concluded that perhaps I really was overreacting and she was more normal than I thought.

Marek was next. He did not get all A's. His grades were lower than Lily's. They looked at each other for a while, a bit confused, then they both said, "That doesn't make sense!" Everyone knew that Lily couldn't tell the difference between a 2 and a 5. She could hardly count in order. I didn't have to tell her that! She knew that! And she knew what was expected. Marek was frustrated and confused knowing he got 100% but did not earn an A.

Their teachers had different grading systems, opinions, and expectations of their students. Marek was a goof-off and didn't have the same respect from his teacher as Lily did. Her teacher saw that she was trying and giving her best effort so graded her according to that. We had to respect the fact that Lily was not the same, but she did not feel honor in her differences.

Of course, as her mother, I considered it all my fault. Perhaps I was giving the boys more attention. So I promised to make sure I was really giving Lily the attention and help she needed in her schoolwork. We put it in the rotation stations and committed ten minutes to each individual being with Mom for homework.

For Lily, we spent those ten minutes on spelling, writing and reading. I corrected her mistakes and we focused until the timer went off. Then I gave her strict instructions to copy the page of spelling words during the next ten-minute session while I was with a brother.

At the end of the ten minutes she brought her paper to me, proud of her accomplishments. Not only was she able to focus for a whole ten minutes, but she actually had completed copying the page. She beamed with pride until I looked at her paper.

Every single thing on the page was written backwards. I took it to the bathroom mirror and held it up. It was perfect. Beautiful penmanship, correctly spelled, perfect in every way. And completely backwards. The entire page was a perfect mirrored image of what it "should" have been.

All of this resulted in a mother studying what her daughter really needed. I released the guilt and blame. Lily was diagnosed with dyslexia. The reason she couldn't tell the difference between 2 and 5 or S, or P, B, Q and so many other letters and numbers, was dyslexia. Her brain was working differently and couldn't decide how to orient things. They were flipped around, upside down, and—my favorite—backwards.

We had already learned from my oldest son's Asperger's—and the experience with Ms. Rose and Brenden—that disabilities come with strengths. We took this knowledge to my daughter's situation. How amazing that she could write backwards! What an amazing gift to be able to see things that others could not! Her creative imagination was off the charts! And this is how our gratitude list for Lily's dyslexia began. In time we were able to find ways to respect and even honor her differences.

This would never work in the real world. Dyslexic people are expected to never be good readers. They typically struggle through school and life, holding themselves back because they have what most people call a learning disability. All the respect in the world wouldn't help her to read, though. So, seeing the ability to read as an essential, base need, we made a choice.

One morning I looked at my daughter, my precious angel on loan from heaven, laying in her bed and clutching her belly, wishing she didn't have to go to school that morning. Her eyes met mine and welled up with tears. I sat on the edge of the bed and she let out a whimper.

"Lily, I have an idea. If you will go to school for the rest of the year without being sick or complaining at all, I will let you be homeschooled next year. There's only about a month left. I think you can do this and I think it will be good for you to learn at home next year. We will focus on getting you to read. What do you think?"

Well, wouldn't you know, her symptoms vanished instantly. She sat up and asked, "Really?"

"Yes. Really."

She wrapped her arms around me in a thankful hug then hurried to get ready for school. She wasn't even late. Her excitement for not having to go to school made her excited to get there that day.

The first thing to do in gaining respect is to create your personal gratitude list. Knowing their base needs can help you see the people in a better light, which will make it easier to create the gratitude list. Likewise, creating the gratitude list can help you discover the base needs.

When base needs are known and conversations can be had about filling the needs, magic happens. It was magical for Lily to be excited about going to school. Knowing base needs takes little more than effort and time. The flip side of this is being too prideful or overindulgent and spoiling the child. You can worry about this if you want to. But we all need to be careful that we are not shutting out greatness.

Being humble means you accept what is given to you, including your gifts of greatness.

Even when they are disguised as a disability.

When Does Everyone Win?

The choice to homeschool Lily was a compromise. Most of the time people think of compromises as a give-and-take scenario. She needs something so I give something, and then she will give something in return. When I told her she could be homeschooled if she went to school happily the rest of the year, it was a compromise. But not in the way you would expect. It was much more than give and take.

A compromise is really a co-promise—a cooperative promise made for the benefit of everyone involved. When we make agreements we should not need to give up important things. I have heard some people say the only way compromising works is when everyone loses something. It doesn't have to be that way in a family.

Making a co-promise is knowing what is needed and wanted—respecting and honoring each other to the point of supporting the progress in each individual. It's a conversation that leaves everyone more hopeful and encouraged. The details are worked out in PPIs and the family works together to help everyone get what they need and want.

Everyone wins. Everyone means Every. One. Each and every individual member of the family contributes to how the family functions and progresses. Every one contributes to the happiness and welfare of everyone else. Seen or unseen, if you are part of a family, you have influence. Then the other members of the family have a choice in response to the influence.

We want our team to win. Our team is our family. We want the entire team to win.

Everyone on the team wins by making and keeping co-promises.

And then we celebrate!

Creating Co-Promises

The co-promise is a fundamental understanding that we are a team. It works hand in hand with the PPI system.

This is my favorite story about success and everyone winning. We have been using the FRAME formula for years now. The stereotype is that teenagers are selfish and don't care about anyone. They won't talk to their parents and all sorts of other negative things. I say these are false. We do not expect that in our family and so far these stereotypes have been proved wrong.

Dallas is now 16 years old. He is just as brainy as ever and even more vocal about his opinions and feelings. We have come so far since he said, "I thought you were going to tell me 17 times." Yet, we have been able to embrace him as an individual. We have overcome the suicidal thoughts and created real self-confidence. We have learned ways to deal with the oppositional defiance.

Dallas came to me late one night and declared he needed a PPI. It was nearing midnight and I was at my wit's end with the day. I have learned I am a morning person and midnight is pushing my limits. So I took a deep breath and said, "Okay, Dallas." We went to the office. I turned my attention to him wondering what he needed. He said, "Hello mother."

I said, "Hi." And expected him to start talking, since he is so good at it. "Hi." I was a little confused and repeated myself. "Hi."

There was a short pause before he said, "How are you today Mom?"

"Dallas, why did you call for a PPI? It's late and I need to get to bed. If you need something, let me know. What do you need?" His answer shocked my system.

"I just haven't seen you yet today and I wanted to visit. How are you?"

Right about now, most people would be wondering how much money he wanted, or what he broke. But I know that Dallas is completely truthful and honest. Since we have our systems in place there is never a need to beat around the bush. He gets complete honesty in return.

"I'm okay. I'm a little frustrated, but I'm okay."

He says in all his wisdom, "Mother, I have noticed you are frustrated and I have a solution for you."

He begins sharing his observations with me. This meeting was called for me! Not him. Bless his heart! He wanted to help me. In my tired brain I kept telling myself not to interrupt and listen. He went on about how I am not getting things done that I have said I was going to do.

When it is my turn, I tell him, "I know I'm not getting things done. I know I have problems and I am not perfect. I know all these things!" I started to hear my voice get louder.

"Mom, you seem upset. I am just letting you know..."

I interrupted him. "Yes, I am upset! You are keeping me up late to tell me all the things I am doing wrong and I already know it!"

"But Mom. You haven't let me finish." His voice was calm and compassionate as he called me out.

"Okay. Get to the point." I was not using the most friendly way of communicating, but I didn't leave and I gave him a chance to be heard. It is vital to stay and listen.

He melted my heart when he said, "Mom, remember. I am here for you. I'm on your team. I got you. I have a solution for you. I think you just need to multitask less. You're trying too hard. It's okay mom. I've got your back. I'm on your team."

I cried openly as he hugged me. He accepted my apology and the next morning I was able to thank him for calling a PPI for me.

My 16-year-old is on my team. We are a family on purpose for a purpose. I have made co-promises with my teenagers and they are there for me as much as I am there for them.

This is why I do coaching and why I wrote this book. Imagine if every parent had their teenagers on their team! Imagine every family, your family, supporting each person as part of a team with love, respect, honesty, and happiness as everyone's end goal.

POP Steps

The foundation for the co-promise goes back to when I made a choice that was the most important decision of my parenting life. I decided I was going to love my children. I decided to love each one of them as individuals. I wanted them to feel loved and appreciated. I chose and made the decision. Decisions are not always easy. I have had people disagree with my having so many kids. The doctors legally had to advise me against carrying quadruplets for the risk it posed to my health and the health of each baby. We decided and chose to carry on the path God placed before us, trusting there must be a way to achieve.

Decisions create trust and are made in trust. Making decisions is the only way to win. When we decide what is wanted then we know when we get to the goal. If you don't know what you want then you will never get it.

So many times people wonder what to have for dinner. Is it this or that? Well, I don't know. What do you want? I don't know either. You choose. And eventually neither one is happy because no one made a decision and time turned into an argument and growling bellies.

I used to get so mad when my husband would not tell me what his favorite food was. Then I learned he just loves food! No matter what I would make him, he loved. When we make that decision to eat an apple instead of the donut, we get to love the apple. If we regret our choice and wish we got to eat the donut, we don't fully enjoy the apple. If we choose the donut, we can enjoy the donut. It's a choice we make. We can respect our choices. Enjoy the donut and eat an apple later. Don't eat while immersing yourself in guilt and regret. No matter how healthy the salad is you will not benefit from it if you are hating every bite.

When I decide to love my children, I decided to love my choice. No matter what mistakes we make along the way, we have decided to love and respect each other. As my husband has often reminded me, "I chose my love, and I love my choice." Living in gratitude is the only way to really live.

NOTES:

NOTES:

CLOSING REMARKS

For my daughter to overcome her dyslexia she needed more balance. Isn't that what we all need? Balance? Seeing how critical it was for my daughter to read we found a mentor for her. It was my first real experience with a person who was there for the sole purpose of helping: seeing what we needed, being painfully honest with us in teaching what needed to be corrected, giving us new information, helping us see things in a different way, and encouraging us to make the changes in our lives to make our end goal possible.

Pat told us she didn't believe in learning disabilities like dyslexia. She said they were all just an imbalance and lack of communicating from one side of the brain to the other. It was a hopeful description that I embraced. Coincidentally this concept is a principle that translates over every relationship. Whether the problem is between brain hemispheres or people, the answer is balance and understanding of exercises to strengthen the weakened parts.

The assignments for her dyslexia were simple and yet complex at the same time. Nearly every exercise involved standing on a balance board and focusing on a task. Really focusing.

Summary of The FRAME Formula Action Steps

There is no such thing as balancing life and business. There is no business. It is all life. Everything is intertwined together and everything affects everything else. You cannot have ice cream for breakfast and feel like you ate a salad. Plans are the first thing needed. Ice cream for breakfast happens when there is no plan.

Here is the plan. I call it the FRAME Formula. It will strengthen and add balance to your family and how you communicate with each other. You can download at copy of the FRAME Formula outline at https://taggarttrainings.com/bonus/frame-formula-outline/

The FRAME Formula

F: Freedom to Speak
- Identify base needs
- Walk down the hierarchy of needs
- Ask: What would support the goal we are hoping to achieve?
- Ask: How can I provide the base level needs?
- *Remember: Safety creates, allows, and supports respect.*

R: Respect and Honor
- Identify the points of view
- Find ways to give sincere compliments by using gratitude lists
- Find common ground by using love lists
- Disagree appropriately
- *Remember: Respect and honor support working together.*

A: Accountability and Action
- Identify action plan
- Empower with acceptance and not playing the blame game
- Create Accomplishment Journals
- Forgive along the way

- Forgiveness hinges on points of view and doors open on hinges
- *Remember: Accountability and Action support making it meaningful.*

M: Make it Meaningful

- If there is no meaning it means nothing.
- Connect and show up
- Create uninterrupted time and focus attention.
- Clear expectations = trust
- Create rotation stations and priority plans
- See the PPI Map in section four and the Outline for The FRAME Formula in section one
- *Remember: When there is meaning, everyone wins.*

E: Everyone Wins!

- Decide! Decide to love them. Make decisions.
- Be happy about decisions.
- Celebrate progress.
- Celebrate your ability to communicate better.
- *Remember: Everyone means Every. One. And you are on the winning team every time you take, make, or give your time to your family.*

Communicate Like It's Your Superpower!

Discovering the FRAME Formula was really a process of becoming an independently united family, primarily with me as the mother accepting that my children are individuals and so am I.

It was a big step for me to take, allowing them their own learning styles and to have their unique ways of communicating. Letting my kids take personal accountability was really accepting that we are different people. Knowing that they need their own time to learn and experience life as their life, not mine. They are not an extension of me in the literal sense. They are a vital part of my life and our paths are eternally woven together. Still, we are different strands in the fabric. Each of our lives has its own beauty to contribute to the whole. When I let them do their own weaving, the outcome is more beautiful than if I tried to control and keep them in the same pattern as my thread.

Their differences make life more complex, challenging, and so much more interesting. The beauty of the weaving is individual growth. The power to change and improve is held within the power of accountability. When we allow and recognize that we are different people, we empower others, including our children. We do not need to hold to the responsibility of making our children be perfect or behave perfectly. We can teach them and allow them to be themselves. Holding onto an imagined responsibility for other people's actions will weigh us down over time. It weighs us down so much because it isn't ours. The idea of perfection must be released, along with the notion that it is achievable, and a parent's responsibility. Our children, although ours, are meant to be individuals with personal goals, thoughts, ideas, motivation, and accountability.

More individuals mean more ideas. More ideas lead to greater possibilities and inventions. Collaborations eliminate waste and improve functionality of the systems, whatever they may be. Every collaboration, when done respectfully, leads to improvements. If nothing else, I can stop saying "I am not an octopus" and let other people use their hands to help, as well as my own.

Our house is still full of loud sounds. They are happy, loving sounds. This week, as six of my kids are now teenagers, we have become even louder. But the sounds are more cooperative, more fun, and incredibly supportive of one another. Today I hope our neighbors hear us. I hope they find joy in our extreme laughter. I hope they will have their hearts touched as much as mine is. And I am sure if they whisper as they pass our house they are sharing a wish that they could have the same love and fun in their homes.

Now you know how we do it. Now you have The FRAME Formula and steps to communicate like it's your superpower, too!

Because, as our children, they are worth it. And as their parents, so are we.

And here is a link to an extra bonus video course. Just click here to request yours: https://taggarttrainings.com/bonus/

NOTES:

NOTES:

THE FRAME FORMULA

Your Parenting Source to Communicate
Like It's Your Superpower!

"Share This Book"

Retail $14.95

Special Quantity Discounts

5-20 Books	$13.95
21-99 Books	$11.50
100-499 Books	$10.25
500-999 Books	$8.95
1000+ Books	$6.95

To Place Your Order Contact:
(801)803-0399
Info@TaggartTrainings.com
www.TaggartTrainings.com

ABOUT THE AUTHOR

LYDIA TAGGART IS ABOUT AS NORMAL as a person you could find, if there were such a thing as normal. She loves to embarrass her kids and test her limits on not being embarrassed by singing and dancing, riding crazy roller coasters, and dreaming about food. As a recovering French fry addict, one of her favorite memories is when one of her sons practically begged her to open a restaurant serving her peanut butter and jelly sandwiches, because they are the best on the planet!

It wasn't always that way though. Her history of burnt almost-everything transformed to beyond delicious sandwiches just like her communication skills and love for her family transformed from crash and burn to confident and connected. She was not always good at anything that she is good at now. She developed systems to improve. And that's why she wrote this book.

The Taggart family grew from the happily married couple, Lydia and her husband, Steve, to include six young children just after the oldest child's fourth birthday. It was an intense learning environment for Lydia. Believing that the greatest calling in the world is your role within the family, and having a solid belief that everything happens for a good reason, Lydia focused her efforts on learning how to communicate with each of her children, including quadruplets, in the best ways possible. This meant learning to communicate with high functioning autism, dyslexia, ADHD, and ODD, just to name a few of the challenges that came along with all those kids.

Taggart's background includes a degree in Family Studies and Psychology, as well as certifications as an NLP Practitioner, Life Coach, Executive Coach, and in Time Dynamics. She uses her experiences to work with parents and show them how to know who they are with confidence. She guides them to collaborate with their family and realize each individual's value and unique contributions to the world.

The parents who hire Lydia are excited to improve communication within their homes. Most come seeking her effective systems and methods which bring you the best results. That's where this book comes in. The FRAME Formula is about communicating in a way that leaves everyone winning, feeling connected, heard, valued, and even when there are disagreements—as we all have—there is still a unified appreciation.

Email Lydia at info@TaggartTrainings.com to receive your free 20 minute consultation and be sure to mention you saw this message in the book.

Special <u>FREE</u> Bonus Gift for <u>YOU</u>!

To help you achieve more success, there are **FREE BONUS RESOURCES** for you at:

TaggartTrainings.com

FREE $1997 VALUE

FREE CONTENT TO
IMPROVE YOUR COMMUNICATING SUPERPOWERS

Get started now at

TaggartTrainings.com

Want More Training?

No More Communication Blinders

Getting You Focused for Success

Lydia Taggart *shares her secrets on how to create your family communication plan...*
AND SHE'S THERE TO COACH YOU!

TAGGART TRAININGS

Private and Group Coaching Available

What the program is:
- Communication skills
- Critical thinking skills
- Relationship skills
- Ways to process emotions

TaggartTrainings.com

Made in the USA
Middletown, DE
26 January 2020

83745160R00056